ZEPHYR

ZEPHYR

poems
by
Quills Literary Club
RBVRR Women's College
Hyderabad

HAWAKAL

HAWAKAL

Published by Hawakal Publishers
33/1/2, K B Sarani, Dum Dum, Kolkata 700080
India

Email info@hawakal.com
Website www.hawakal.com

First edition December, 2019

Cover photograph: Canva
Cover design: Bitan Chakraborty

ISBN: 978-93-87883-96-3

Price: 150 INR | USD 6.99

R.B.V.R.R Women's College (Autonomous)
Narayanguda, Hyderabad
Re-accredited by NAAC with
B++ Grade (4 Cycle)
Recognized by UGC as
College with Potential for Excellence

Quills Literary Club
Department of English and Foreign Languages
RBVRR Women's College
Narayanguda, Hyderabad-500029
Telangana

Editor's Note

"Poetry is just the evidence of life. If your life
is burning well, then poetry is just the ash."
Leonard Cohen, *The Paris Review,* 2016

The above words by poet, song writer,
Leonard Cohen has found a recurrent space in
my academic and creative pursuits. They have
often lit fire in my usually dull life.

"Zephyr," is the spark, I have been
looking for since a long time. I have been the
chief editor of thequilsclub.blogspot.com since
its inception in December, 2015 and always
wanted to bring out a book of poems by
members of the Quills Literary Club. This
chapbook is only a small step towards the many
beautiful adventures the girls of our club will
embark on in future. It is an eclectic collection
of poems that will make you laugh, cry, wonder,
question and long for the poet in you. These
poems have been written over the years and
many of them already published by the blog.
However, a printed book is always a joy to

behold. This project would not have been possible without the kind consideration of Hawakal Publishers, Kolkata, one of the most esteemed independent publication houses in India. I thank poet Kiriti Sengupta and writer, publisher Bitan Chakraborty for sparing their valuable time for us. It is a matter of extreme privilege and honour for us to associate with Hawakal Publishers.

The book would not have been possible without the support of our college Secretary cum Correspondent, Prof. G. Sudarshan Reddy; Secretary, HMVS, Prof. K. Muthyam Reddy and other eminent members of our College Management. I thank Principal, Dr K. Sarada for her encouragement. I thank Ms Grace Sudhir, former head of the department and our previous colleagues who played a key role in founding the club and encouraging the blog. Immense gratitude to the Head, Department of English, Chairperson, Quills Literary Club, Ms M. Suchitra Reddy for her constant guidance, love and enthusiasm. I thank my colleagues, Dr Sumitra Jaiswal, Ms K. Anupama, Ms Amroze Mehdi, Ms Y. Jayanthi, Ms Bhagvati Putcha, Ms Mercy Rani, Ms Pranitha Martand, Ms Neha Jaiswal, Ms Ruth Kezia and Ms P. Sandhya. I thank student editor of the club, A. Mounika for her timely help.

I thank the contributors and appreciate their participation with prompt submissions. *Zephyr* is a small yet, a vivacious effort towards the emotional empowerment and evolution of young women of Telangana.

May we write more! May we thrive more!

Dr. Jhilam Chattaraj
Assistant Professor
Department of English and Foreign Languages

Preface

Poetry is when an emotion has found its thought and the thought has found words.

Robert Frost

I congratulate all the young poets of R.B.V.R.R.Women's College for having put up this book. It is a commendable effort which is appreciated.

The Department of English, RBVRR Women's college initiated the Quills Literary Club to promote academic, critical and creative thinking among young students through, debates, presentations, flash drama and dramatic performances. We aim to enhance the creative writing skills among students of our club.

There is an intrinsic interest in the question regarding the ways the poets of emerging generation take into their hands, an art as a starter for discussion, a pleasure that responds greatly if you give time. The strong shade of feelings that exist in every poem comes alive and meanings appear unexpectedly under meanings; prose is chopped conveniently into lines for writing free verse.

I am grateful for the book you have in your hands now, it reveals a whole new generation of exceptionally talented and differently talented poets. This is not a collection of fanciful lyrics or disassociated rambles, but voices that speak, ponder, puzzle and alert our impulses that often remain unspoken. The poems in this anthology mark spontaneity and energy of a new kind.

I thank all the members of the Department of English for their help, cooperation, and encouragement to enhance and exhibit the skills hidden within the students.

I thank Dr. Jhilam Chattaraj, Coordinator, and Editor of the blog of the Quills Literary Club, for her continuous effort in motivating the students to write their thoughts and create a world of words.

Poetry is a deal of joy and pain and wonder with a dash of the dictionary.

Khalil Gibran

Ms. M. Suchitra Reddy
Head
Department Of English and Foreign Languages
Chairperson
Quills Literary Club

Quills Literary Club

The Department of English, RBVRR Women's College, Hyderabad established the Quills Literary Club on 15 December, 2015. The aim of the club is to provide a safe space for students to share their literary and creative ideas. The Club aims to fulfil the vision and mission of the College by enhancing the ability of the students to communicate in the larger social and cultural context. The Literary Club is named *Quills* as the humble quill was used by our early writers to pen some of the greatest Classics of Literature. It is also an identity marker of English literary writing and pays homage to its beginnings in the annals of history and poetic thought.

Each month, we organise a meeting. The meetings include discussions on specific literary text, author, cultural issues and even films. Students make presentations, conduct debates, perform skits, dance drama, stand-ups on the decided topics.

The club also organises, workshops and guest lecturers for the members.

The club encourages students to participate in various literary and cultural competitions held in the city.

The club has the writing portal, *Quills: The World of Words.*
http://thequillsclub.blogspot.com/.com
The blog was introduced to encourage creative writing among students both from rural and urban areas.

Achievements
Conducted workshop on "Flash Fiction," 15 December, 2015.

Conducted workshop on Theatre Arts by actor Rathna Shekar Reddy, 13-15 December, 2016.

Blog Entry, " Spills to Remember you by" by Student, Juveria Tabassum selected among

top eight in "Blogathon Contest", organized by Women's Web, Juggernaut Books, June 2017.

Students win prizes at "Performing Texts,' a competition by UGC and Osmania University, August, 2017.

Students selected as Volunteers for Hyderabad Literary Festival, 2018.

Nominated by India Reading Olympiad as one of the Best Reading Clubs in India.

Members

Chair Person: *Ms. M. Suchitra*
Coordinator: *Dr. Jhilam Chattaraj*
Organising Secretary/Treasurer: *Dr. Sumitra Jaiswal*
Member: *Ms. Anupama.K*
Member: *Ms. Amroze Mehdi*
Member: *Dr. Y. Jayanthi*
Member: *Ms. Mercy Rani*
Member: *Dr. Bhagavati Putcha*
Member: *Ms. Pranitha Martand*
Member: *Ms. Neha Jaiswal*
Member: *Ms. Ruth Kezia*
Member: *Ms. P. Sandhya*
Student Editor: *A. Mounika*, BA III Year

CONTRIBUTORS

T. ABHIRUPA
MSC II Year

Don't Complain

In middle of the city, there might be a person,
alone and waiting for a soothing hand.

A couple, in some corner of the country
is trying to welcome a new member in the family.

Across the lane, there might be a person,
who is hungry for a handful of rice.

At the border of a country, there might be a soldier,
waiting for the beloved.

Everyone has their own enemy in the battle of life.

So, don't complain about what you lack;
Feel blessed for what you hold.

L. AISHWARYA
BA I Year

We

We,
the two arms of a compass
can never be separated.

No matter how far we go,
we, the two bowls of a balance
can never weigh alone.

No matter how light things are,
we, the two bonds of matter
can never be broken.

No matter how tough our fights are,
we, the two rosy lips of a baby girl
can smile forever and ever.

No matter how pricking the pains are,
we, like the dance and the dancer will remain together.

ANISHA BODAPATI
BTCFS II Year

The One that Slipped away

She slipped away from my embrace
as I tried to hold on.

Her image dissipating as though smoke
leaving me helpless and alone.

I looked through the tears, and in the distance
I found her crouching, smiling and at peace.

The solace she found I could not find
for I felt the pain she refused to feel.

The smile on her face was far from comforting
It chilled my bones; but I did love her.

So, I strove to reach her, to hold her
but my legs were chained to the solid ground.

The ground that held me back, slipped away from her,
the light was drawn away from her eyes
by the void of pitch black; but the light
wasn't of her eyes, it was of my life.

ANUPAMA.K
Assistant Professor
Department of English and Foreign Languages

Discipline

Discipline, your name scares me.
Just a mention of the word sends
ripples of fear through the brain.

We know you are the devil of our delight,
never do we realize the pleasure
we   can treasure if only we train
and tune our minds.

Most of us see you as our foe
but the one who gets adapted to you, creates wonders.

This is the misery and mystery that cannot unfold you.
In fact, you demand nothing
and create space for everything.
Yet, we are terrified to be with you.

ASFIA KHANAM
BTCFS III Year

Mirror

It's me here telling you the truth.
Don't try to get people's *ruth*.

You are not what you actually should be.
You show the face which you want the world to see.

Your life is a dream for the people out there.
Life is just a game, be fair.

You try to be the person you compare yourself with.
You are playing a role which is a part of your life's skit.

Just be the person you are.
Twinkle in your own way, you are a star.

Be yourself, no matter what it takes.
You will overcome all your fears and aches.

I have shown the mirror, it's in front of you.
What you actually are, you already knew.

Listen to your heart and what it says.
Show the world your original face.

DR. BHAGAVATHI DHARBA
Assistant Professor
Department of English and Foreign Languages

They are mine

My thoughts are dancing to
the melodious tunes of my heart
to reach someone to understand my deepest emotions.

But those emotions have sunk in satirical notes
and ridiculous narrations,
they are considered useless and many said 'of no value.'

But they are mine, and my own thoughts,
searching to find their destiny.

Though my search is endless,
my joy too would be endless
if those empty spaces are filled.

They are mine, my own emotions.
To those emotions,
I've become a slave, they flash in my life like seasons.

Neither I know, nor I thought that
like the monsoon, my heart is shedding tears for you.

Summer is magnanimous
and has its enchanting beauty,
flashing its heat, and I am in a dilemma to discover

whether the heat is generated through the
distance that I travelled in search of you.

My thoughts are flowing like waves.

My emotions are drowning in search
of the pearls of your love in the depths of my heart.

My feelings are drenching in my own tears.
Those melodies unheard by you
got sick of being alone, talking to self.

Going back to nostalgia, I found no one but myself
all the time, only myself.

DEEKSHA REDDY
FNBC III Year

All about Life

Life, you are a question
and I shall answer you with will and courage.

Every day, something new,
some surprise, but

I shall
face them all
and not fall.

One wise man once said,
"there is no hope without fear and no fear
without hope."

I fear, I may fail and lose
but I shall try and try to the last
and be brave.

No, No, I shall never quit
I will pursue life
with love, joy and grit.

JUVERIA TABASSUM
BCOM III Year

Spills to Remember You by

She lifts her eyes.
Meets those of the stranger in the mirror.

Watches-
as a shaking hand lifts itself.

Probes-
a fresh gash under her lip.

Coagulation
of fresh blood and old questions.

She searches the stranger's face for answers-
silence.

A whole year of bewildering silence.

The class jester had fallen in love-
and love, it turned out, was no joke.
She tried, for a while,
to drown out the tears of the present
with symphonies of past laughter-

But when flesh and bones are stained every night,
how can memory stay untouched?

"The jester is dead," says the stranger in the mirror.
"Not quite," she smirks,
wide, hard, until the laughter refuses to stop;
her wound splits open.

Now, she raises her own hand,
dips a finger in the red,
smears across the mirror.

"The joke's on you, dear lover,
"jesters never die."

She recalls walking out,
as she walks onto the stage.
"Some stand-up comedians," she says,
"have to sometimes stand up for their lives."

KEZIA RUTH
Assistant Professor
Department of English and Foreign Languages

Le Papa LOUP ?

Mon Cher Papa,
J'ai peur de perdre des gens
Que j'aime profondément,
Mais parfois, je me demande ......
Y a-t-il quelqu'un qui a peur de me perdre ?

En vérité, oui, c'est toi Mon Papa !
Comme un loup,
La grâce de marcher en group,
La beauté d'enseigner les petits,
Ne jamais quitter la troupe,
Ne jamais reculer sauf pour laisser une
empreinte.

Oh Mon Cher Papa, Ce que j'aime en toi,
Je me sens bon, je me sens ohh !
Je me sens forte, je me sens un roi,
Quand je marche â côte de toi.

MEERA SAHEBA
BTCFS II Year

I Grow Up

From parents holding my hands,
to my parents leaving my hands,
I grow up.

From having low self-esteem,
to showing the world my confidence,
I grow up.

From realizing that I need to be unique,
to realizing that I'm indeed unique;
I grow up.

From thinking that I was hopeless,
to inspiring people around me;
I grow up.

From focusing on my scars
to loving the same scars;
I grow up.

From fighting with myself endlessly,
to fighting the people who mess with me;
I grow up.

From finding inspiration in my role models,
to finding inspiration even from kids;
I grow up.

And realizing that before loving others,
I need to love myself first;
I grow up.

A MOUNICA
BA III Year

The Stardust Palette

The clock strikes twelve
and I try to see the stars beyond the dusty air,
shining on their own against a dark canvas.

I paint my canvas the same dark hue,
hoping I make stars of my own.

Excited, hopeful and motivated,
I dip my paintbrush in stardust;

I'll make my stars bleed purple,
for it's my canvas.

The clock strikes one
and the brush slips from my fingers.

Anxiety peeks through the cracks in my paint;
and I rush to perfect my stars.

The real ones take millennia to form,
humans do not have the same luxury.

I paint them over and over again,
my fingers shake and I grow frantic,
desperate to create my own bright star.

The clock strikes two
and suddenly the canvas looks bleak.

The dark colour has an ominous feel to it,
and my mind chokes me with the same darkness.

My brush pauses, I try to recall why I started;
I look up, and I can't see the stars anymore.

Why shine if you fade at the break of the dawn?
Why rush to live if death is the destiny?
The brush slips again; this time I don't pick it up.

NIKITHA
BTCFS III Year

The Unforgettable College Days

I have made friends and memories
that will last forever in my mind.

I have learnt the lessons that will mould
me into the person I will find.

I have discovered the possibilities of
choices that I will need to make,
wondered about the challenges that lie on
whatever path I take.

Listening to my heart, I set a course
for the goals I wish to achieve;
and now I begin the journey of my dreams
knowing that all I need, is to believe.

It's time to say goodbye.
My journey here has come to an end.

I've made some cherished memories
with all my college friends.

We've watched each other learn and grow
and change from day to day.

I hope that all the things we've done
will help us along the way.

So, it's with happy memories
I go out the door;
with great hope and expectations
for what the next year holds in store.

PRIYANKA DUBEY
MZC II Year

On Friendship

Friendship is a roller coaster of highs and lows.
Some friends can't stay apart nor wish to be torn.

Some struggle to rescue their drowned liaisons
and some cheer on their comrades from afar:

They come in gangs of geeks and clique of jocks
they are partners in crime and peas of a pod.

They stand firm and brave against the harsh waves,
trusting and leaning on each other to hold tight.

They think they're invincible against all charges
yet, they wobble and sway against the test of time.

Opportunities knock at their doors and hearts change,
priorities re-arrange and promises long forgotten.

Friendships are crazy pacts and silly ties,
so easily tossed away in the hurdles of life.

Yet, some few and true friendships never fade
still standing side by side against the harsh winds.

RITHIKA VARAM
MZC III Year

Shirts

The touch of his washed shirt on my skin,
removes the traces of the ones that never fit me.

The remnants of my father's cologne on the shirt,
gives me hope that tomorrow will be better.

The frayed ends of that shirt,
helps me pick up my scattered confidence.

And, the feel of the shirt swallowing me up,
reminds me that I still have a place called home.

RITU SARDA
MZC II Year

Unmasked

Wandering round the clock in the dark,
I've practiced putting on a deceiving mask.

It is too late to reach for the light
until the end, all I'm doing is fight.

Every effort I put in, seems to be less
every cry for help I scream, useless.

I stand up again... I brace my soul,
the voice in my head is hard to ignore.

K. RUCHITHA
BBA III Year

My Unseen Agony

You see me
joyfully singing and gliding in the sky.

You see me
without shackles and living my best life.

You see me
flying high as if to touch the moon and the sun.

You see me
crossing borders and dancing with the wind.

You do not see
my struggle for survival as I fly to escape reality.

You do not see
my monsters lurking in the shadows to catch me.

You do not see
that I cannot trust to be tied down anywhere.

You do not see,
how I dance and sing to relieve my burdens.

Yet, you see me
singing from my heart with wondrous joy.

Yet, you see me
splashing in the fountains without a care.

Yet, you see me
waking up with the sun and fluttering about.

Yet you see me,
living my fullest to spread love and peace.

SRILEKHA SAGAR
BCOM III Year

On Suffering

The word ends with a ring,
during which the resolve swings.

Two sides of the same person fight,
victory depends on the person's might.

Suffering is encountered by every person,
some have it shallow, some have it deep.

The tenure of suffering might be bitter,
but it serves as a bad thought emitter.

Suffering can be physical or mental,
but never losing hope is vital.

It may be sorrowful,
so, you need to be careful.

To end suffering you may swallow poison,
but that is a fake medication.

You should try to cope,
for if you try, you can see the sun.

SUPRIYA KIRAN
BCOM III Year

Celie Love

I again wrote to God about this baffle.
Maybe, it seemed to him a trifle.

I lost the hope,
didn't try to cope.

On one fine day
my eyes met her sparkling eyes:

Eyes full of love
Eyes full of care

The moment paused,
I found my letters answered.

The eyes made me realize my worth,
now, I no longer accept what is put forth.

I realized love was not Albert,
love was Shug. "Shug Avery,"
who made me live life in my way.

She made my life,
I made her my wife.
Now I carry love in my bones,
light in my smile.

Now, I'm not silly,
only Celie "happy Celie."

SYEDA MARIYA
BA I Year

Once Upon a Blue Moon Night

Once upon a blue moon night,
I was walking down the George Street by the moonlight.

Far, very far, there up, very high,
the stars twinkled like sparks in the sky.

I had a feeling, a creepy one, that I wasn't alone,
there was something unusual in the cold wind's tone.

My feet tightly dug in the ground,
not a third soul could be found.

Standing behind the old Banyan tree,
I noticed someone staring at me!

I called her, asked "Who art thou?"
"You got these wounds, when? how?"

She had beautiful eyes- deep, dark, bold,
but somehow I felt something was untold.

"What is your name?", She said, "Grace,"

I smiled at her and took her to my place.

"At daybreak, I'll leave you at your house," I said,
she quietly had her supper and went to bed.

At dawn, I searched for that damsel of fifteen,
but to my surprise, she was nowhere to be seen.

I went to Uncle David and told him the tale,
by and by, I noticed, his face grew pale.

"That girl? Grace?", he was taken aback,
"She died a decade ago in a terrorist attack."

The words of Uncle David fell like lightning,
the thought of her were very frightening.

Years have passed, but I still fear that blue moon night,
when I was walking the George Street by the moonlight.

TAHREEN FATIMA
BTCFS II Year

Car of My Choice

My heart pounds fast like a Ferrari,
and seeing your picture makes my day a luxury.

Eyes run through the crowd, looking for you,
like a shining BMW.

Lips like a Lamborghini,
keep speaking about you freely.

Brain works like a Mercedes,
and writing about you is done with ease.

Even a Limousine is too small,
for all my feelings to go in it all.

Like the B in the logo of a Bentley,
My dreams fly constantly.

Like the headlights of a Jaguar,
my wish of meeting you shines bright each hour.

Like a funky Bugatti,
and a matte black Audi,
my hope blooms like a flower.

Be it a Range Rover, or a Land Rover;
be it a Porsche, or a Rolls Royce-
Your heart is the only car of my choice!

L. VEDA SRI
BA II Year

Contraries

You are my inspiration,
the soul of my verse,
but the pain you have given me,
is no less than a curse.

You are my dream,
the one I strove hard to achieve.
But you're like a star in the sky,
that I could never seem to reach.

You are my light,
that once shone so bright.
But you left me in plight,
and there's nothing left in my sight.

You are my poem,
that I recite day and night.
But I never knew you abhorred reading,
Until you made my words hide.